Starting and Running a Small Trucking Company

An Easy Step by Step Guide to Starting and Running a Small Trucking Company

By Elizabeth King

ISBN-13:978-1530859504

ISBN-10:1530859506

Printed in the United States of America.

Table of Contents

Introduction

First, welcome to your new journey. Not every truck driver can or will start their own trucking company. But you have decided to, so let's get you on the right road.

The trucking industry is no different than any other business, with one exception, it's stronger. Yes, I said it, but think about it. Everything that every person purchases is hauled on a big truck, ship or rail.

Most trucking companies fail with in the first 7 months, why? Mostly because they are not prepared for what the road has for them.

It is my intention to pave that road for you, the driver, the wife, that wants to be one your own but aren't quite sure how to do it successfully.

So, let's get started.

Elizabeth
CEO / Loaded Up N Truckn

Chapter One

Start Up Cost

Alright, so you have a bright idea, or your wife has a bright idea to no longer give away money from your hard work and being away from your family for sometimes weeks at a time. Now what?

Let's start with making a plan, listing what you will need to have to get started. Some of this will depend on your credit score, unfortunately that is where our world is heading, everything leans on credit score.

1. Authority $300-600

    As of Oct 2016 companies will have to pay $300 for their MC or motor carrier number AND $300 for the DOT or department of transportation number for the state you will operate in

2. Insurance $6000-12,000

3. Company setup $250-1200

4. Fuel - 1 week $1000

    Most fuel cards will bill weekly, so you have almost two weeks to start paying.

5. Maintenance-1st mo. $180 – 300

    Oil changes typically cost up to $300, you'll need one about every six weeks

6. Truck letters $90

7. UCR $79

    You'll need to apply for the UCR (Unified Carrier Registration) prior to going to get your truck plate

    https://www.ucr.in.gov/ucr/apps/ucrAcctDetails.action

8. IRP/Truck plate $1600

    Plate amount depends on what time of the year you are starting, they will prorate.

9. 2290 $550 annual

    This will be pro-rated if you start your company mid-year, this will be needed in order to get your truck plate

10. BOC3 $30-200

You'll need this right after you apply for your authority, this is the designation of process agents, that cover every state in case you have trouble and need someone to represent you. Type in BOC3 and you'll find a list of companies that offer this service. **WARNING once you apply for your authority, your phone will ring off the hook with companies trying to provide their services, choose to use them or I'll show you how to save literally hundreds of dollars doing yourself**

11. Loadboards $15-60

Most Loadboards will give you a week or ten days free

Total amount needed to get started and running:
$ 9400- 16,850

Business Plan

Putting together a business plan can be simple as a few pages showing what you want to do, how you're going to get started and what your one or three-year plan is for the future of your company.

Most business plans are used to obtain financial backing from banks or even family members. Other business plans can be used to help show the future plan of your company.

Here are some tips in creating a simple business plan:

1. One-line description of your company, service offered
2. Financial model: Start-up cost; expenses, income (potential) *see below for sample*
3. Opportunity: what need will your company going to meet? (transportation of goods, food, etc.)
4. Milestones: Finding/purchasing truck, obtaining authority, ins, etc., opening company date, getting freight
5. Business operation – what tools and resources will you use to run your company? Loadboards to find loads, QuickBooks or something like that for accounting, Truckingoffice.com to track loads/dispatching/invoicing/IFTA miles are just a few tools you'll want to look into using.
6. Why are you qualified to succeed – years in industry, this is like your resume
7. Competition – choose 2 of your competitors and list their strengths and weaknesses

Example:

Business Plan

A. Introduction

1. **Name of Company:** _____ **Contact Number:** _____

    Name of Applicant: _____
    (Please provide photo identification with your application)

2. **Is this a new or existing business?**

    ❏ New   ❏ Existing   Date business established: _____

3. **Type of Operation:**

    ❏ Manufacturing   ❏ Wholesale/Retail

    ❏ Agriculture   ❏ Construction

    ❏ Aquaculture / Fishing   ❏ Transportation

    ❏ Forestry   ❏ Mining

    ❏ Tourism   ❏ Other (Specify) _____

4. **Mailing Address:** _____

    Postal Code: _____

5. **Telephone Numbers:**   Residence: _____ Cell: _____

                             Fax: _____ E-mail: _____

6. **Proposed location of business:** _____

7. **Legal Form of Business:**

    ❏ Incorporated   ❏ Sole Proprietorship

    ❏ Partnership   ❏ Co-operative

    ❏ To be incorporated

Projected Business Expenses

How much capital are you planning to invest in starting up your trucking company? Also, try to forecast the financial requirements for the first year.

Particulars	Start-up	3 months	6 months	12 months
Authority				
Insurance				
UCR – Unified Carrier Registration				
BOC3				
Legal form of business				
Fuel				
Truck letters				
Loadboards				
Accounting/Office Software				

Notes

Chapter Two

What's next? Paperwork

Authority

Yes, sadly the next step is paperwork, and trust me there is quite a bit of it.

You'll start by going to FMCSA website, click on registration and Getting started:

https://www.fmcsa.dot.gov/registration/getting-started

Here they show you the steps of the registration process.

You can apply for your MC and DOT numbers online.

**Remember to keep your PIN when you first start the application, you'll use this over and over again.

Kentucky

If you go will travel through Kentucky, you'll need to obtain a Kentucky number as well. These numbers will also go on your truck along with your MC/DOT/VIN. Check that out at:

http://transportation.ky.gov/Motor-Carriers/Pages/Commercial-Motor-Vehicle-Credentials.aspx

New Mexico

New Mexico is an interesting state, and very confusing. You'll need a permit to travel into that state either before you go into the state or you can get at the weight station.

I would call before signing up on the below website, to make sure you obtain the proper permit.

https://tap.state.nm.us/tap/_/

After you apply for your authority

After you've applied for your authority, one your phone will ring off the hook with companies offering services to provide you with what is necessary for FMCSA to approve your application. These services include the BOC3 filing and compliance in regards to drivers, like your drivers file and drug/alcohol testing and company policy. But, I'll show you how to do that yourself if you wish to save money, otherwise the choice will be yours to choose one of the many companies that will be calling you.

BOC3

There are many companies that offer services for just this need. BOC3 is a form that is needed to be filed with FMCSA after you've applied, this is a list of processing agents for every state in the US that represent your company if the need arises.

Do a google search of BOC3 and a list of companies will appear. I used www.aprocessagents.com purely because of the price. A friend that started his trucking company at the same time choose not to use them because their customer service team seemed to have been hired in another country.

Insurance

Once you've applied for your authority, you have a short period of time to obtain insurance and have the insurance company file the MCS90 form to FMCSA.

When you are first starting out, it's hard to find a good company because most trucking start-ups close their doors with in the first eight months which makes it hard for the one's that will make it.

If you join a trucking association, they typically offer truck insurance or can guide you to a company.

You'll also get lots of calls about this as well and mail regarding insurance.

We used Rig quote, their customer service was excellent and when I told them the budget we had, they found a way to meet it.

Legal Company Setup

This next part is going to be up to you, whether you have no intentions of growing and just want to have your own authority so maybe a DBA (doing business as) works for you. Some may have big dreams about growing and adding trucks and drivers over the next five years to definitely a corporation is the way you should look at going. There's also a LLC which is great for growing companies as well, there are some tax advantages to this form compared to a corporation.

I would suggest discussing with your spouse or accountant to determine what is best for you.

Here are the definitions of each form of legal setup:

Doing Business As: DBAs are also known as Fictitious Names, Fictitious Business Names, Assumed Names, and Trade Names. Essentially, a DBA is the name of a business other than the owner's name or, in the case of a corporation, a name that is different from the legal or true corporate name as on file with the Secretary of State

Corporation: a company or group of people authorized to act as a single entity (legally a person) and recognized as such in law.

LLC: A limited liability company (**LLC**) is the United States-specific form of a private limited company. It is a business structure that combines the pass-through taxation of a partnership or sole proprietorship with the limited liability of a corporation.

Tax ID Number / FEIN

Even if you are a DBA and everything else is under your social security number, you will have to have a tax id number from the IRS. You will need this for the form 2290 in order to get your truck plate and renew your plate. You will also need the EIN if you go into New Mexico.

2290

The 2290 is the heavy road tax needed to obtain your truck plate and in some states needed for a permit to travel into that state.

You can print the IRS form from the IRS website and complete yourself, of there are a few online companies that will submit this to the IRS for you.

TIN / EIN

You can apply for your tax id or employer identification number online at the IRS website:

https://www.irs.gov/Businesses/Small-Businesses-&-Self-Employed/Apply-for-an-Employer-Identification-Number-(EIN)-Online

Notes

Chapter Three

Fuel Cards

There are many options of which fuel card to apply for. Depending on what part of the country you will spend most of your time, could determine whether you go with Wright Express, Fuelman, FleetOne or go directly to the fuel station like with Kangaroo or Pilot.

Each company offers a discount, whether at the pump, when you are billed or quarterly.

There are a variety of ways of being billed and paying. Most companies will set you up on auto draft, or give you a login to their website and you control when you pay them.

*Warning, if you don't pay the bill they will freeze your account and turn off your card until paid.

To Factor or Not

I wish I knew what I'm about to tell you when I first started. Most brokers, if you decide to go that way to get started, have their own in house factoring they will reduce your final payment by if you choose to use them.

There are many, many factoring companies out there and again they will call you once you've applied for your authority.

Because we started with brokers that paid within one to seven days from the delivery of the load, we choose not to factor with an outside company. But again, that's something to discuss with your spouse or partner.

GPS

Unfortunately, we got suckered into getting a Nextraq GPS when we first started, I was reviewing so many contracts that I missed it was a three-year contract. Nextraq is great, for bigger companies and if you have more than yourself or husband driving. But I wouldn't waste the money upfront on this service. I'd admit, it was awesome to be able to log into the website and see exactly where my husband was, but not necessary for a startup company. It was supposed to also help with IFTA miles, it tracked them but I need another program to track the fuel we purchased and the states we bought fuel in, so it was a waste of money for us.

Drivewyze / Prepass

Drivewyze is a great tool to use, it's an application on your smartphone and helps you go pass scale houses. Simple download, pay monthly and when you are getting close to the scales you will be directed to either pass through or pull in. It will depend on what state you are in, not all are on the program yet.

IFTA / IRP

Typically, these two serve in the same office and under the Department of Transportation.

IRP is an account you'll need to setup when you get your truck plate. You'll also need to file the 2290, Heavy Road Tax in order to get your plate. And, don't forget the UCR, if you don't have when you go to the IRP office, you'll have to go back. And the wait time at these offices, is brutal, so just be prepared for half a day there.

IFTA is the fuel tax that you will have to file every quarter. Some states offer the ability to calculate online, then you complete the form. You can also hire someone to do this for you if you aren't accounting mind like. The IFTA office will tell you if you did it wrong, some are nice like South Carolina and call you while other states like Tennessee just send a nasty letter.

Software Needs

If you want to run your business correctly, I would suggest getting a QuickBooks, Quicken, or Money program to keep track of where your money is going. This will be helpful when you file taxes. You can get an old fashion disk or some offer online programs.

Truckingoffice.com I found very helpful and inexpensive. This program allows you to track your fuel cost, dispatch your loads and invoice. You can run reports for IFTA or year end.

There are many Loadboards to choose from. A few we went with, and I tried at least a dozen were: 123loadboard.com, Truckstop.com and UShip. But it will also depend on what type of freight you will haul because there is hotshots.com for truck doing that, hot shots. Or there's centraldispatch.com for auto haulers. So really, just surf the web, talk to truckers and do some homework.

Notes

Chapter Four

Don't Waste Your Money

Here are a few items I found that really wasted our money.

1. Business cards – although they are cheap, I never have given one out
2. Website – some Loadboards will give you a free website with your membership with them. Although Go Daddy.com offers a great start up price, I got our website for $12 for the first year but it went to $180 the next. Then I saw that 1123loadboard have me one FREE and they did all the work.

Necessary Marketing Tools

I search high and low for a list of direct shippers. If you have will pull a reefer or van trailer, here's a company that has just that list. We called, hundreds of farms/nurseries but finally after a few weeks we had them sending us email blast of loads they needed covered. I would recommend Produce Universe or also known as the Red Book. You can pay upfront or monthly but well worth the money.

Don't grow too fast

I'm not saying this just from a budget stand point but it sends up red flags if a new trucking company grows too fast. I would personally suggest staying at one truck for at least a year.

Notes

Chapter Five

Equipment

If you don't already have a truck/tractor and trailer, your next big purchase will be just that.

Something to keep in mind if your new to the industry is that there are laws that are changing the trucking industry. Like, the latest that will implement electronic logging for all trucks, with the exception of trucks made prior to 1999. There already is a huge demand for older trucks because of this new law in place and that will begin right around the corner in 2017. So if you are looking for a new rig, keep the new law in mind. Some driver doesn't care about electronic logs, but the old school drivers are used to paper and would rather stay that way. The call is all yours.

In reference to the trailer you will pull, are you looking at rates or what you know? Two years ago the rates for a flatbed trailer were very high, some drivers said they were making $5 per mile. However, they are not the same as of 2016, they are lower. You can't go wrong with a reefer unit, especially during the winter months, you'll haul a lot of potatoes during the winter with a reefer. And not to mention it'll also be handy in the summer if you are hauling plants.

Also consider the length of the trailer, we had a 48-foot reefer, but when the reefer unit went down it was hard finding van loads for a 48 foot. We recently sold our 48 foot and upgraded so to speak to a 53-foot reefer.

Finding Freight – Broker vs Shipper

Let's start with this comment, unless you already have contacts with direct shippers, I would start with a few brokers. Yes, you are giving them money you could be earning, but if you build your company and network with other drivers make connections, then in no time you'll be hauling direct with shippers.

A broker takes on a lot of the logistics so to speak. You will call, negotiate a rate and accept. Then they send you everything you need, rate agreement, driver instructions and the shipper will have the paperwork you need.

Here are a few of my favorite brokers we dealt with, based on broker relations and pay method:

Allen Lund, Coyote, XPO, GIX and TTS

After these brokers I would say TQL would be next, but be very careful of them. We had a claim we had to pay out of our own pocket because their shipper claimed our driver was allowed on the dock to count what was being loaded but that was not the case, and since our driver did not have the shipper write 'shipper load and count' on the bill of lading, when he delivered and it was short, even though the seal was intact, we were the ones that owed for the missing freight. I considered not paying TQL and just ignoring them, but being a new company at the time and not wanting to go through litigation, we paid them but made a company policy on any TQL load that the shipper would always write 'shipper load and count' to protect us in the future. Lesson learned!

Now, on to shippers. Like I mentioned early, they are hard to find. You can't just type into google 'direct shipper', I've tried. I finally found the Red book, after months of searching and they were a great contact. I did try to contact big companies like Kroger, Walmart, etc. but they typically have a minimum of 10 or even 50 trucks per trucking company to haul for them. That's why brokers are in business, to bring the shipper and carrier (that's you, the trucking company) together.

Notes

Chapter Six

Drivers, DOT Regulation, Vehicle maintenance

As a wife of a truck driver with over twenty years' experience on the road, I didn't know what I was getting into when we started our own company in 2014. One thing I was unclear of was all that was needed to have on file for the driver, or drivers and what the DOT regulation says.

You'll need a file for each driver that includes the following DRIVER QUALIFICATION FILE

1. Employment application
2. Safety performance history record request (below)
3. Motor Vehicle report – MVR (last 3 years)
4. Annual review of MVR/driving record (below)
5. Driver certification of violations (below)
6. Road test (below)
7. Medical certificate
8. Driver daily logs (these can be purchased at truck stops)
9. Vehicle maintenance records (below); NOTE it is not enough just to keep receipts, the FMCSA requires you to record when parts are installed. You can use a simple notebook or I've attached a sample form
10. Pre-employment and random drug test participation and results.

You will need to have a drug/alcohol policy in force as well. I've attached a sample copy of such policy.

SAFETY PERFORMANCE HISTORY RECORDS REQUEST

SECTION 1   AUTHORIZATION

I, (Print Name) _____ , hereby authorize:

(First, M.I., Last)

Previous Employer: _____   Email: _____

Street Address: _____   Phone: _____

City, State, Zip: _____   Fax: _____

to release and forward the information requested by section 3 of this document concerning my Alcohol and Controlled

Substance Testing records within the previous 3 years from_____

                                         (Date of Employment Application)

to:

Prospective Employer: _____   Attn.: _____

Street Address: _____   Phone: _____

City, State, Zip: _____

In compliance with 49 CFR §§40.25(g) and 391.23(h), release of this information must be made in a written form that ensures confidentiality, such as fax, email, or letter.

Prospective employer's confidential fax number:_____

Prospective employer's confidential email:_____

_____   _____

Applicant's Signature   Date

This information is being requested in compliance with 49 CFR §§ 40.25 and 391.23.

SECTION 2   ACCIDENT HISTORY

The applicant named above was employed by us. ☐ Yes ☐ No

Employed as _____ from (mm/yy) _____ to (mm/yy) _____.

Did he/she drive motor vehicle for you? ☐ Yes ☐ No If yes, what type? ☐ Straight Truck ☐ Tractor/Semitrailer
☐ Bus   ☐ Cargo Tank   ☐ Doubles/Triples ☐ Other (Specify) _____

ACCIDENTS: Complete the following for any accidents included on your accident registrar (§390.15(b)) that involved the applicant in the 3 years prior to the application date shown above, or check here ☐ if there is no accident register data for this driver.

Date	Location	No. of Injuries	No. of Fatalities	Hazmat Spill
1._____	_____	_____	_____	_____
2._____	_____	_____	_____	_____
3._____	_____	_____	_____	_____

Please provide information concerning any other accidents involving the applicant that were reported to government agencies or insurers or retained under internal company policies: _____

_____

_____

Signature:_____

Title: _____ Date:_____

PREVIOUS EMPLOYER – COMPLETE SIDE 2, SECTION 3

SECTION 3	DRUG AND ALCOHOL HISTORY

If driver was not subject to Department of Transportation testing requirements while employed by this employer, please check here ☐.

	YES	NO
1. Has this person had an alcohol test with a result of 0.04 or higher alcohol concentration?	☐	☐
2. Has this person tested positive or adulterated or substituted a test specimen for controlled substances?	☐	☐
3. Has this person refused to submit to post-accident, random, reasonable suspicion, or follow-up alcohol or controlled substance test?	☐	☐
4. Has this person committed other violations of Subpart B or Part 382 or Part 40?	☐	☐
5. If this person has violated a DOT drug and alcohol regulation, did this person fail to undertake or or complete a program prescribed by a Substance Abuse Professional (SAP) in your employ If yes, please end documentation back with this form.	☐	☐
6. For a driver who successfully completed a SAP's rehabilitation referral and remained in your employ, did this driver subsequently have an alcohol test result of 0.04 or greater, a verified positive drug test, or refuse to be tested?	☐	☐

In answering these questions, include any required DOT drug or alcohol testing information obtained from prior previous employers in the previous 3 years prior to the application date shown on side 1.

Name: _____

Company: _____

Street: _____

City, State, Zip: _____ Phone: _____

Section 3 completed by (Signature)_____ Date:_____

SECTION 4	MODE OF COMMUNICATION

This form was sent to previous employer via (check one) ☐ Fax ☐ Mail ☐ Email ☐ Other _____

By _____ Date:_____

SECTION 5	RECEIPT INFORMATION

Complete the following when the requested information is obtained.

Information received from_____

Recorded by:_____ Method: ☐ Fax ☐ Mail ☐ Email ☐ Phone

Date:_____ ☐ Other _____

INSTRUCTIONS FOR COMPLETING THE SAFETY PERFORMANCE HISTORY RECORDS REQUEST

SIDE 1 SECTION 1: *Prospective Employee*

- Complete the information required in this section
- Sign and date
- Submit to the prospective employer

SIDE 1 SECTION 2: *Previous Employer*

- Complete the information required in this section
- Sign and date
- Turn form over to complete SIDE 2 SECTION 3

SIDE 2 SECTION 3: *Previous Employer*

- Complete the information required in this section
- Sign and date
- Return to prospective employer

SIDE 2 SECTION 4: *Prospective Employer*

- Verify that prospective employee has correctly completed SIDE 1 SECTION 1

- Complete the information required in this section
- Make a copy of this form and keep it on file
- Send to previous employer

SIDE 2 SECTION 5: *Prospective Employer*

- Record receipt of the information in SECTION 5
- Keep form on file for duration of the driver's employment and for three years thereafter

U. S. DEPARTMENT OF TRANSPORTATION
MOTOR CARRIER SAFETY PROGRAM
ANNUAL REVIEW OF DRIVING RECORD
(49 CFR 391.25)

Name of Motor Carrier: _____

_____   _____
(Name of driver)   (Social Security Number)

This day I reviewed the driving record of the above named driver in accordance with CFR 391.25 of the Motor Carrier Safety Regulations. I considered any evidence that the driver has violated applicable provisions of the MCS Regulations and the Hazardous Materials Regulations. I considered the driver's accident record and any evidence that he/she has violated laws governing the operation of motor vehicles, and gave great weight to violations, such as speeding, reckless driving and operation while under the influence of alcohol or drugs, that indicate that the driver has exhibited a disregard for the safety of the public. Having done the above, I find that

[ ] The driver meets the minimum requirements for safe driving, or

[ ] The driver is disqualified to drive a motor vehicle pursuant to CFR 391.15

_____   _____
Date of review   Reviewed by: Signature and Title

MOTOR VEHICLE DRIVER
CERTIFICATION OF VIOLATIONS 391.27

I CERTIFY THAT THE FOLLOWING IS A TRUE AND COMPLETE LIST OF TRAFFIC VIOLATIONS (other than parking violations) FOR WHICH I HAVE BEEN CONVICTED OF OR FORFEITED BOND OR COLLATERAL DURING THE PAST 12 MONTHS.

DATE	OFFENSE	LOCATION	TYPE VEHICLE OPERATED
_____	_____	_____	_____
_____	_____	_____	_____
_____	_____	_____	_____
_____	_____	_____	_____
_____	_____	_____	_____
_____	_____	_____	_____
_____	_____	_____	_____
_____	_____	_____	_____
_____	_____	_____	_____

If no violations are listed above, I certify that I have not been convicted or forfeited bond or collateral on account of any violation required to be listed during the past 12 months.

_____   _____
(Date of Certification)   (Driver's Signature)

_____   _____
(Carrier's Name)   (Motor Carrier's Address)

_____   _____
(Reviewed by: Signature)   (Title)

CERTIFICATE OF DRIVER'S ROAD TEST

Instructions: If the road test is successfully completed, the person who gave it shall complete a certificate of the driver's road test. The original or a copy of the certificate shall be retained in the employing motor carrier's driver qualification file of the person examined and a copy given to the person who was examined. (49CFR 391.31 (e) (f) (g).

CERTIFICATION OF DRIVER ROAD TEST

Driver Name _____

Social Security Number _____

Operator or Chauffeur's License Number _____

State _____

Type of Power Unit _____

Type of Trailer _____

If passenger Carrier, Type of Bus _____

THIS IS TO CERTIFY THAT THE ABOVE NAMED DRIVER WAS GIVEN A ROAD TEST UNDER MY SUPERVISION ON _____, 20____, CONSISTING OF APPROXIMATELY _____

MILES OF DRIVING. IT IS MY CONSIDERED OPINION THAT THIS DRIVER POSSESSES SUFFICIENT DRIVING SKILL TO OPERATE SAFELY THE TYPE OF COMMERCIAL VEHICLE LISTED ABOVE.

_____   _____
(SIGNATURE OF EXAMINER)   (TITLE)

_____
(ORGANIZATION AND ADDRESS OF EXAMINER)

Inspection, Repair & Maintenance Record

VEHICLE IDENTIFICATION

MAKE	SERIAL NUMBER
YEAR	TIRE SIZE
COMPANY NUMBER/OTHER I.D.	OWNER, IF LEASED

DATE: . MILEAGE   **OPERATION PERFORMED, INSPECTION OR REPAIRS**

Model Substance Abuse Policy

I pledge that my company will take reasonable action to create and maintain a workplace free from substance abuse. My company will work to increase awareness of the dangers of substance abuse within our workplace and throughout the construction industry.

TABLE OF CONTENTS

SCOPE OF POLICY

This document contains procedures for implementing a drug and alcohol testing program at the *Company*. The company prohibits the use, possession, sale, purchase, manufacture, distribution, transfer or consumption of alcohol and all illegal drugs, including legally regulated drugs.

This program applies to all employees and potential employees of the company, as well as subcontractors at all tiers, including non-bargaining and bargaining unit employees.

DEFINITIONS

Banned Substances: Illegal substances, as defined by federal/state laws, including:

        a. Amphetamines
        b. Opiates
        c. Phencyclidine (PCP)
        d. Cocaine
        e. THC (Marijuana/Cannabinoids)
        f. Intoxicants (drug and alcohol)
        g. Synthetic drugs

Third-Party Administrator: The company may retain a third-party administrator to perform testing and reporting procedures. See Appendix A: Additional Definitions.

POLICIES AND PROCEDURES

A urine drug screen shall be administered under the following circumstances.

1. **Pre-Hire Drug Screening**. All potential employees must submit to a urine drug screen no later than the commencement of employment. Pre-hire drug screening will test for the presence of illegal drugs and substances and the illegal use of prescription drugs. This screen does not include an alcohol test. Potential employees who refuse to submit to this test will not be permitted to work for the company.

If the employer participates in a pre-screen/certification program through a collective bargaining agreement (CBA) or other arrangement, and the potential employee has undergone a prior screening to which, through the CBA or other arrangement, the company is provided access to the results/certification, then the potential employee shall be deemed to have complied with the company's pre-hire drug screening requirements.

2. **Existing Employees**. Existing employees who are transferred from another location must submit to a urine drug screen prior to entering the jobsite. This screen tests for the presence of illegal drugs and substances and the illegal use of prescription drugs. This screen does not include an alcohol test. Employees who refuse to submit to this test will not be permitted to work for the company.

If the employer participates in a pre-screen/certification program through a CBA or other arrangement, and the employee has undergone a prior screening to which the company has access to the results/certification, then the employee shall be deemed to have complied with the company's pre-hire drug screening requirements. Likewise, if an employee has undergone a urine drug screen with the company within the previous three (3) months, and the company deems this test sufficient, then the employee shall be deemed to have complied with the company's pre-hire drug screening requirements.

3. **Testing for Cause**. All employees may be tested for cause when a reasonable suspicion exists that the employee appears to be under the influence of illegal drugs or illegally using prescription drugs, synthetic drugs and/or alcohol.

4. **Causal/Incident-Related.** All employees who are involved with, or may have contributed to, an incident that results in property damage or requires treatment beyond onsite first aid are required to submit to a drug screen and alcohol test. (Note: a company may also require a drug screen and/or alcohol test for incidents resulting in first aid treatment. Please consult your state/local laws pertaining to testing procedures to verify if such a practice is permissible).

5. **Random.** When permitted by law, employees may be randomly selected for unannounced drug and alcohol screening using a scientifically/statistically valid computerized number generation process. Employees are notified of selection no more than 48 hours prior to testing.

6. **Reinstatement, Return-to-Duty and Follow-Up Testing.** After signing an agreement or participating in substance abuse counseling established by the company, the employee must complete a drug screen before returning to active employment.

TESTING PROCEDURES

I. Drug Screening of Applicants for Employment

1. Upon entering the jobsite or workplace, all applicants will proceed to the project office or trailer. They will be advised whether specimen collection will occur onsite in an approved facility or at an approved clinic offsite.

2. Each applicant will read and sign a Drug Screen Consent Form prior to any test being administered.

3. On a pre-printed, itemized form furnished by the employer, each applicant will be asked to identify any medication he/she is taking or has taken during the 30 days preceding the test.

4. A formal chain of custody will be established for every drug screen.

5. A split sample consisting of two urine collection containers sealed in a plastic container will be furnished to the applicant. (Note: Testing may be performed by a third-party administrator.) The containers must contain an amount of urine sufficient for one

Enzyme Medical Immunoassay Test (EMIT) and two Gas Chromatography/Mass Spectrometry (GC/MS) tests (no less than 2 ounces of urine per container). Each applicant's urine specimen will be collected and temperature tested for verification. The second container will be used in the event the first container becomes contaminated.

6. Before the specimen leaves the applicant's sight, the urine containers will be sealed with security tape that has been initialed by applicant.

7. Specimens collected onsite will be transported to a laboratory in accordance with the chain of custody procedures. A portion of the sample will be tested using the EMIT; if positive, another portion and/or the split sample will be tested for verification using the GC/MS test.

8. The remainder of the urine specimen and split sample will remain at the laboratory for 30 days following the test.

9. Upon signing a form giving consent to use the urine sample for drug screening, the applicant is eligible for employment on a 72-hour probationary basis. This consent form is co-signed by the collection specialist.

10. Any applicant who refuses to submit to a drug screening will not be eligible for employment.

11. The employer receives the drug test results within 72 hours. If the applicant's test results in a confirmed positive, as confirmed by a medical review officer (MRO), he/she will be terminated immediately and paid for all hours worked, if permissible by state/local law. The individual will not be eligible for employment with the employer for a period to be determined by the employer, not exceeding one year. If hired later by the employer, and contingent on a negative drug screen, the employee may be tested periodically without notice for a period of up to one year from the date of hire.

12. If any individual who has tested positive by the MRO wants to confirm the results of the GC/MS test, he/she may do so by having a GC/MS test performed on the previously collected split urine specimen at a certified National Institute on Drug Abuse (NIDA) or Substance Abuse and Mental Health Services Administration (SAMHSA) laboratory of his/her choice. The specimen will be shipped directly from the employer's lab to the lab of the employee's choice. The costs of this test will be borne by the employee. If the results of this test are negative, the individual will be reinstated with full back pay and benefits, and will be reimbursed for the cost of the test. The individual must exercise the option of a second GC/MS test within 24 hours of being notified of the positive results.

13. Pre hire drug screens include tests for at least the following (a five-panel drug screen):

    a) Amphetamines
    b) Opiates
    c) Phencyclidine (PCP)
    d) Cocaine
    e) THC (Marijuana/Cannabinoids)

The company reserves the right to administer testing for additional substances (For more information on seven-panel, 10-panel, 12-panel and hair follicle tests, refer to the "Best

Practices" section of the Construction Coalition for a Drug- and Alcohol-Free Workplace website at www.drugfreeconstruction.org).

II. Drug Screening of Transferred Employees

The procedure for testing employees transferred from another jobsite is the same as the pre-hire procedure.

III. "For Cause" Testing Procedures

1. All employees working for the company may be tested for illegal drugs, substances, synthetic drugs and alcohol if there is reasonable suspicion that the employee is under the influence of alcohol, any of the substances identified in paragraph 13 or abuse of prescription medication. For the purpose of this program, the term "reasonable suspicion" shall be defined as "aberrant behavior or unusual on-duty behavior of an individual employee who:

    (a)   is observed on duty by either the employee's immediate supervisor, higher ranking employee, or other managerial personnel who have been trained to recognize the symptoms of drug abuse, impairment or intoxication (observations shall be documented by the observers);

    (b)   exhibits the type of behavior that shows accepted symptoms of intoxication or impairment caused by controlled substances or alcohol or addiction to or dependence upon said controlled substances; and

    (c)   such conduct cannot reasonably be explained by other causes such as fatigue, lack of sleep, side effect of prescription or over-the-counter medications, illness, reaction to noxious fumes or smoke.

2. Testing of this type will not be conducted without the written approval of the company's superintendent or designated manager. The jobsite superintendent or designated manager must document in writing who is to be tested and why the test was ordered, including the specific objective facts constituting reasonable suspicion leading to the test being ordered, and the name of any source(s) of this information. One copy of this document shall be given to the employee before he/she is required to be tested. After receiving a copy of the document, the affected employee shall be given enough time to read the document.

3. When a supervisor, higher ranking employee or other managerial personnel has reasonable suspicion to believe an employee is using, consuming or under the influence of an alcoholic beverage, non-prescription controlled substance (other than over-the-counter medication), and/or non-prescribed narcotic drug while on duty, that person will notify the jobsite superintendent or designated manager for the purpose of observation and confirmation of the employee's condition. The employee will be given an opportunity to explain his/her condition, such as reaction to a prescribed drug, fatigue, lack of sleep, exposure to noxious fumes, reaction to over-the-counter medication or illness. If, after this explanation, the jobsite superintendent or designated manager continues to have

reasonable suspicion that the employee is using, consuming and/or under the influence of an alcoholic beverage, non-prescribed controlled substance or non-prescribed narcotic while on duty, then, by a written order signed by the superintendent or designated manager, the employee may be ordered to immediately submit to a drug and alcohol screen. Refusal to submit to testing after being ordered to do so may result in disciplinary action up to and including discharge.

4. Employee drug screens for cause will include testing for alcohol, as well as the same drugs as the pre-hire screening test. Each employee will read and execute a consent form prior to any test being administered. Failure to execute the consent form will result in termination.

5. Reasonable suspicion testing shall be performed at a NIDA/SAMHSA-approved clinic. The individual will be immediately accompanied to the clinic by a company representative. Samples will be taken as per the pre-hire procedure.

6. An EMIT test and, if positive, a confirming GC/MS test, will be performed on the urine sample. The remainder of the sample and the split sample will be stored at the laboratory for 30 days.

7. If an employee's test is positive, his/her employment will be terminated immediately. The employee will be given a copy of the results of the drug screen. He/she may have the second container tested at his/her own expense as per the pre-hire procedure.

8. Alcohol detection will be based on an evidential breath alcohol device approved by the National Highway Traffic Safety Act. If an employee's test results indicate he/she is legally intoxicated at or above the state of jurisdiction's legal limit, he/she may be subject to discipline up to and including discharge.

IV. Causal/Incident-Related Testing

Subject to applicable law and consistent with reasonable suspicion, the company reserves the right to require its employees to present themselves for testing within 24 hours following an employee's involvement in an accident, near accident or an incident resulting in lost work time, property damage, and/or injury to any employee or other person while on the company's premises, on the job or otherwise working for the company.

V. Random Testing

Subject to applicable law, the company reserves the right to require its employees to present themselves for random, unannounced testing. The company will adopt an objective procedure, using a statistically valid number generation process, to randomly select employees to be tested. Upon anonymous selection, the company will notify the employee(s) to report immediately for drug testing. The company solely determines the time and frequency of random drug tests. Any employee may be selected for random testing in accordance with state/local laws. An employee could be randomly selected for testing more than once a year.

VI. Reinstatement, Return-to-Duty and Follow-Up Testing/Rehabilitation Programs

The company maintains a referral relationship with drug and alcohol abuse services. Additionally, certain health insurance benefits may provide help to employees who suffer from substance abuse and/or other personal or emotional problems; however, it is the responsibility of each employee to seek necessary professional assistance before alcohol and drug problems lead to disciplinary action.

If the company mandates a sponsored rehabilitation program, the employee will be subjected to a drug screen following the procedures outlined in Section I (Drug Screening of Applicants for Employment) prior to reinstatement. In addition, per post-rehabilitation program monitoring guidelines, the company may subject the employee to follow-up testing for a period to be determined in cooperation with the rehabilitation program and employer. Testing will follow the procedures outlined in Section V (Random Testing).

VII. Drug and Alcohol Testing Requirements for Employees with a Commercial Driver's License (CDL)

The United States Department of Transportation (DOT) requires that all employees maintaining a CDL and operating commercial motor vehicles be subjected to the drug screen policies outlined in the "Testing Procedures" section of this document. CDL employees, per the DOT, are required to submit to a minimum five-panel drug screen for the presence of:

1. Amphetamines
2. Opiates
3. Phencyclidine (PCP)
4. Cocaine
5. THC (Marijuana/Cannabinoids)

A positive test result requires the employee to be immediately removed from operating any commercial motor vehicles on public roadways. In addition, employees whose test produces a positive result must complete return-to-duty and follow-up testing after completion of an approved rehabilitation program as prescribed by a substance abuse professional. Follow-up testing must include a minimum of six unannounced, directly observed drug screens within 12 months of the initial return-to-duty screen following the procedures outlined in Section V (Random Testing).

For more information on the DOT's CDL drug screening requirements, visit:
http://www.fmcsa.dot.gov/documents/Drug_Alcohol_Test_Brochure2009_508compliant_rev2.pdf

VIII. Disciplinary Policies and Procedures

For examples of disciplinary procedures and appeals processes, visit the "Best Practices" section of the Construction Coalition for a Drug- and Alcohol-Free Workplace website at www.drugfreeconstruction.com.

First Offense

Disciplinary actions defined by the company.

Second Offense

Disciplinary actions defined by the company.

Appealing Disciplinary Action

Appeals process defined by the company.

Substance Abuse Rehabilitation

Following a positive result, the company retains the right to enter the employee into an approved substance abuse rehabilitation program. Upon completion of the program, the employee will be subjected to drug screening procedures outlined in Section VI (Reinstatement, Return-to-Duty and Follow-Up Testing/Rehabilitation Programs).

IX. Policy Amendments

Review Procedures

The company will undertake a comprehensive review of the policy biennially. A review panel consisting of senior management, safety professionals and site employees will assess the relevance and current status of the policy's components, as well as incorporate updated procedures and requirements that will ensure the policy meets or exceeds industry requirements. Any policy changes made as a result of the review will be made available and provided to every employee as an addendum to the company's Employment Policies and Procedures Handbook.

In addition to the biennial policy update, the company may undertake revisions due to new regulatory requirements. Any revisions made outside the biennial review will be provided as a separate addendum to all employees.

X. Confidentiality Statement

Employee information, including drug screen results and rehabilitative programs, will be treated as medical records and will remain strictly confidential following HIPAA guidelines for patient confidentiality. Employee requests to release the results of drug screens to any party outside the company must be made in writing and given to the employee's immediate supervisor and designated safety and health officer.

SAMPLE CONSENT FORM

Pre Hire

_____ Release form for obtaining urine samples for drug screening and permission to furnish the results to the company.

For Cause

_____ Release form for obtaining urine samples for drug screening and permission to furnish the results to the company.

_____ Release form for obtaining NHTSA-approved evidential breath alcohol test and permission to furnish the results to the company.

Post Incident

_____ Release form for obtaining test samples for drug and alcohol screening following any incident requiring medical care.

I hereby authorize the _Company_, its physicians or agents, to take the indicated sample from me to use for the purposes indicated above. I understand why these samples are being requested and I give permission for the results to be released to the company and to my employer (if different).

I further release and hold harmless the owner, the company and its subcontractors from any consequences arising out of the drug and/or alcohol test or results therefrom.

_____   _____

Name   (please print)   Social Security Number

_____   _____

Signature (required)   Date

_____   _____

Street   City   State   Zip

_____

Phone Number (with area code)

_____   _____

Witness   Date

_____   _____

Employer   Occupation

DRIVER'S DAILY LOG

(24 HOURS)

Month _____ Day _____ Year _____

Signed - Fill in hours entered
Replaces - Driver returns to his/her possession for eight days

Total Miles Driving Today _____

Total Mileage Today _____

Name of Carrier or Carriers _____

Main Office Address _____

Home Terminal Address _____

I certify these entries are true and correct.

Truck/Tractor and Trailer Numbers or
License Plate(s) / State (show each unit)

Driver's Full Signature _____

Co-Driver's Name _____

	MID-NIGHT	1	2	3	4	5	6	7	8	9	10	11	NOON	1	2	3	4	5	6	7	8	9	10	11	TOTAL HOURS
1. OFF DUTY																									
2. SLEEPER BERTH																									
3. DRIVING																									
4. ON DUTY (NOT DRIVING)																									

REMARKS

SHIPPING DOCUMENTS:

B/L or Manifest No.

Shipper & Commodity

Enter name of place you reported and where released from work and when and where each change of duty occurred.

From: _____ To: _____

USE TIME STANDARD AT HOME TERMINAL

© Copyright 2013 & Publishing by J. J. KELLER & ASSOCIATES, INC.®

DRIVER'S VEHICLE INSPECTION REPORT

AS REQUIRED BY THE D.O.T. FEDERAL MOTOR CARRIER SAFETY REGULATIONS I SUBMIT THE FOLLOWING:

DATE: _____   TRACTOR/TRUCK NO.: _____   TRAILER(S) NO.(S): _____

☐ I DETECT NO DEFECT OR DEFICIENCY IN THIS MOTOR VEHICLE AS WOULD BE LIKELY TO AFFECT THE SAFETY OF ITS OPERATION OR RESULT IN ITS MECHANICAL BREAKDOWN

☐ I DETECT THE FOLLOWING DEFECTS OR DEFICIENCIES IN THIS MOTOR VEHICLE AS WOULD BE LIKELY TO AFFECT THE SAFETY OF ITS OPERATION OR RESULT IN ITS MECHANICAL BREAKDOWN

INDICATE WHETHER DEFECTS ARE ON TRACTOR/TRUCK OR TRAILER - DESCRIBE DEFECT IN DETAIL. USE BACK SIDE IF NECESSARY.

DRIVER'S SIGNATURE: _____

☐ ABOVE DEFECTS CORRECTED

☐ ABOVE DEFECTS NEED NOT BE CORRECTED FOR SAFE OPERATION OF VEHICLE

MECHANIC'S SIGNATURE: _____   DRIVER'S SIGNATURE: _____   DATE: _____

© Copyright 2013 J. J. KELLER & ASSOCIATES, INC. ® Neenah, WI • USA • (800) 327-6868 • Printed in the United States

1-66/79 (Rev. 9/13)

Pre-employment and Random Drug Program

Every driver will need to take a pre-employment drug test and random drug/alcohol test.

There are many, many options of what company to go through to setup your drug program needed by DOT regulations. Most will also provide the necessary supervisory training you will need to complete as well if your spouse or someone else is helping you run the company or you have more than one driver.

Just do a google search and many companies come up. We used our local Workforce Essentials program through our community workforce office. I prefer to support our local companies versus a big company that is based in another state. But that's just me and you have a choice of what you want to do.

Owner Operators Vs Company Drivers

An owner operator is one that owns his own truck/tractor and possibly trailer but wants to use your authority. Typically, a carrier, that's you, will bring on an OO at a certain percentage that goes to him and the rest to the company to cover overhead expenses. The OO would be responsible for his/her own fuel, insurance and maintenance of his equipment. An OO/owner operator usually makes 80-85% of the load.

On the other hand, a company driver would get a certain amount per mile and the carrier covers all the overhead like fuel and maintenance expenses. Typically, carriers pay drivers between $ .35 - .50 depending on experience.

You should have a contract in either situation stipulating how you will pay the driver and how you will take your percentage. Be very careful with this part because some carriers take their cut then take out the fuel and insurance but their contract says they will take out the fuel and insurance and then take out their cut. In this case, the carrier was making more money and in essence stealing from the driver.

Here's an example:

	Taking % before expenses	Taking % after expenses
Revenue	$2000	$2000
15%	-300	
Fuel	$500	$500
Insurance	$500	$500
Subtotal	$700	$1000
15%		-$150
Total to driver	**$700**	**$850**

Notes

Chapter Seven

What to expect the first year

Your first year will be filled with ups and downs.

What you deal with will depend on what part of the country you are hauling for, what time of the year you start your company and what you are hauling.

Overall, the peak season for this industry starts in March and goes until about the end of October, that is when you will find the best rates for moving freight. During the off peak months, November to February, you will find cheap freight all over the country and no matter what type of equipment you are using.

We typically shut down, or run part time during the off peak season. In the future, we will be closed two weeks around Christmas and the entire week of Thanksgiving. Shippers typically are not hauling during this time and freight is hard to find.

Safety Audit

Within your first year of business, you will have to complete a safety audit. This will vary state to state as how they perform the audit. You may receive an email to go online, like South Carolina does, and submit all your paperwork via an online portal, then DOT will contact you as soon as it is complete to advise if you passed or failed. Or, like Tennessee, you may get a phone call to go to the closest highway patrol office to perform the audit. Currently in TN, there are three locations due to several officers retiring recently, I had to drive two hours for our audit.

The safety audit is to make sure you are running your company like FMCSA and DOT regulate. You'll need to provide the following to them:

1. Company information (what you completed on the FMCSA application)
2. Driver list (see below)
   a. Current and terminated
3. Driver qualification files (list above in chapter six)
4. Alcohol/drug company policy (sample above)
5. Pre-employment and random drug test results and drug program contract
6. Daily log books – they will pull at random one month to review
7. Driver payroll records
8. Driver supporting documents (trip reports, expense records, fuel, toll, scales)
9. Vehicle accident files
10. Vehicle list (make, model, year, VIN) (see below)
11. Vehicle maintenance records
12. Driver vehicle inspection reports (does not apply to one truck operation)
13. Company gross revenue for last full year

14. Total fleet mileage for last full four quarters
15. Form MCS-90 from your insurance company on the current policy

When you get the call or email about the safety audit, they will send you a list of what they need.

The following will help make sure you are prepared when the call comes.

The safety audit is pass or fail, they are looking to make sure you are running the company as you should. If you fail, they will keep a sharp eye on you moving forward and you will have to rectify whatever you failed.

They have several criteria that sends up red flags. They watch the DOT inspections and companies that are shut down. If you do anything out of line, let's say your driver gets shut down over and over for log book entry, that will give them a red flag. Or if you have a driver that has several accidents in a year, that will give them a red flag and the next step would be for them to knock on your door and dig even deeper into your files.

So, keep your nose clean, and you should only hear from them once to perform the safety audit.

Company Data:

USDOT Number: _____

Company name: _____

List all drivers in past 365 days, include company/leased/owner operators:

Driver list for _____ **(carrier)**

Driver Name, Driver's license number, Date of hire, Full/Part time, Termination date

    1. _____
       _____

    2. _____
       _____

Vehicle list for _____ **(carrier)**

Vehicle year, Make, Company unit#, VIN, GVWR

    1. _____
       _____

    2. _____
       _____

List of corporate offices and date of incorporation:

_____

List of all cargo hauled, include hazardous materials:

_____

List number of accidents in past year: _____

List the total fleet mileage for past four quarters: _____

List Gross Revenue for last full fiscal year: _____ for fiscal year ending ____

Company email: _____

Federal Tax ID Number: _____

Above reported by: _____ _____ _____
                  (Name)   (Title)   (Date)

Conclusion

Well, that's all I've got to share with you. I hope you found this book useful and easy to help you with starting up and running your new trucking company.

I welcome you to the industry and wish you much success in this new adventure for you.

I'd love to hear from you, how helpful this book was, how easy it was to use to get you started and your story.

Feel free to share by sending me an email at:

evadesante@gmail.com

Thanks and God Bless!

Made in the USA
Middletown, DE
11 July 2018